Taking the
Classroom
Into the
Community

Taking the
Classroom
Into the
Community

A Guidebook

Neal A. Glasgow

CORWIN PRESS, INC.
A Sage Publications Company
Thousand Oaks, California

For information address:

Corwin Press, Inc.
A Sage Publications Company
2455 Teller Road
Thousand Oaks, California 91320
e-mail: order@corwin.sagepub.com

SAGE Publications Ltd.
6 Bonhill Street
London EC2A 4PU
United Kingdom

SAGE Publications India Pvt. Ltd.
M-32 Market
Greater Kailash I
New Delhi 110 048 India

Printed in the United States of America

Library of Congress Cataloging-in-Publication Data

Glasgow, Neal A.
    Taking the classroom into the community : a guidebook / Neal A.
Glasgow.
        p.   cm.
    ISBN 0-8039-6478-1 (cloth : alk. paper). — ISBN 0-8039-6479-X
(pbk. : alk. paper)
        1. Community education—United States—Handbooks, manuals, etc.
    2. Community and school—United States—Handbooks, manuals, etc.
    3. Mentoring in education—United States—Handbooks, manuals, etc.
    4. Portfolios in education—United States—Handbooks, manuals, etc.
    I. Title.
    LC1036.5.G53   1996
    370.19'31—dc20   96-15307

96 97 98 99 00 10 9 8 7 6 5 4 3 2 1

Corwin Press Production Editor: S. Marlene Head

Contents

Preface

Many educators see the need to connect colleges and universities, community professionals, businesses, and other community resources to secondary schools and classroom curricula in new, cooperative relationships. How to accomplish this and determining what roles each will play remain the biggest obstacles among those willing to make the attempt. There are large gaps between a willing philosophy for participating in such a program and the working models, concrete protocols, and examples of successful programs necessary to include large numbers of students in community learning activities. This book has been written to bridge these gaps and provide educators, community businesses, public agencies, professionals, and program designers with examples of an existing working model that has successfully integrated the community and higher education into secondary school curricula.

How can the community—the real world outside the academic classroom—become a greater educational asset for students, teachers, and schools? The community around most secondary schools contains businesses, public agencies, colleges and universities, and a range of professionals with many resources that can enhance and contribute to a student's educational success within and outside the classroom walls. By extending the classroom into the community, students begin to see that learning can and does occur in the abstract "real world" outside their classroom, and that schoolwork and continuing to learn are really important in solving everyday problems and completing tasks in all levels of life within their own community. For most, it is a necessity of a successful professional life. For many students, connecting to a community program within a more traditional curriculum offers them new reasons for continuing their education. Furthermore, it creates added interest, motivation, and, for some, a new purpose and dedication for and to learning.

Trade schools or specialty schools that are created to train students to enter a specific job or trade have a built-in relevance. Students are there to learn the exact skills and knowledge to allow them to do a job. Within these schools, learning pathways, curricula, and pedagogy directly contribute to working literacy in a targeted area. This clarity of purpose does not exist in many secondary school academic classroom settings. The type of learning experienced by many students in secondary schools relates only to the specific unit, narrow subject topic, or book chapter, and it is applied during some type of contrived test situation. In athletics, practices, training, and preparation are very relevant and authentic in that they will be applied in a game or match many times in front of authentic audiences. In secondary schools today, the connections between the academic classroom curriculum and a student's world outside the classroom are not that clear.

Academic curricula can be created or modified to use new resources, and secondary schools and the community can begin to look at each other with new eyes as new, innovative opportunities for students are created, designed, developed, and implemented. Connections between academic curricula and authentic application can be forged.

This book breaks down one school's experience in expanding the role that the community can play in offering students new educational opportunities. A specialized academic community program offers clarification and creation of greater context in how academic classroom experiences will apply to the student's life outside his or her secondary school classroom by using resources available in most communities. This model includes connecting the student to the reality of the prerequisites for many careers in which they may be interested, the need for further preparation in colleges and universities, and a clear view of the potential of many professions or careers. Connecting the curriculum to the reality of the outside world is difficult. When real-world problems, collected and brought by mentors within the students' own community, become part of the classroom curriculum, a new view of learning is fostered. Abstract concepts, principles, facts, and techniques come alive as the students apply what they learn within authentic problems and settings.

How can the community—the real world outside the academic classroom—become a greater educational asset for students, teachers, and schools? It can do so by becoming co-collaborators in the development of new educational opportunities for students. The information you will be reading may be a model you can use or it may act as a trigger to creative relationships of your own. Within this book are working examples of mentored relationships—their structure, management, assessment, and evaluation. The book also addresses some of the problems of these types of interactions, such as recruitment of mentors, the liability for those leaving campus, and curricular justification for programs such as these. Each chapter, from "Is There Room for Something New?" to "The Changing Roles for Teachers," describes the real concerns that have been expressed by those wanting to develop curricula and activities that use community educational pathways within their classrooms. The information within these chapters contains philosophy but, more important, goes beyond philosophy by providing concrete protocols and real examples from a program that has successfully used community connections.

About the Author

Neal Glasgow has taught and been involved for 12 years in instruction program design at the middle school, junior high, and high school levels. He cofounded and currently teaches in a small, specialized, self-contained school-within-a-school emphasizing science, math, and technology in northern California. The smaller specialized school is located within a larger restructuring high school, and Glasgow has been involved in the development of instructional programs and curricular design for both schools. The school is widely known and recognized for its innovative instructional programs, especially its award-winning community mentor program. It has received recognition as a runner-up for the State of California School Board Association's Golden Bell Award and received Sonoma State University's and Sonoma County Department of Education's Jack London Award for innovation and excellence in education. Its community mentor program has received many inquiries and visitors over the years and was the focus for a 1993 television program called *Classrooms of the Future.*

Glasgow has spoken and provided seminars locally, regionally, and nationally on many aspects of educational program design. He is the author of two other books on learning and teaching strategies and curricular design: *Doing Science: Innovative Curriculum for the Life Sciences* and *Inspiring Learn-*

ing: A Guidebook for Problem-Based Instruction. His main goal is the creation of curricular activities that engage students in the most motivating, interesting, and valid curriculum possible.

Introduction

A science teacher would love to connect his or her enthu-
siastic biology students to a working laboratory in a local college. A principal speaks at a local business roundtable,
and a retired newspaper writer and a businessperson offer
to volunteer in her high school. A group of history students
wants to get credit for its contact with a local attorney and
together visit the local courthouse and watch an authentic
trial. A school district administrator views a grant application that calls for networking with various community agencies to develop an interactive program. Most of us would
agree that connecting the biology students to the laboratory,
the volunteers with teachers and classrooms, the students to
the courthouse, and the administrator to other agencies interested in education would provide potentially powerful
educational opportunities and experiences. How do you
make such connections part of the classroom curriculum?

The problems in fostering contacts such as these seem
overwhelming. The science teacher could make the contact
but does not know what exactly to ask for or how to manage
such a program. The principal hands a note describing the
writer's and the businessperson's requests to a couple of
teachers. The history teacher says it would not be fair to give
the students credit for their courtroom experience when he
could not give the opportunity to all of his students. The

administrator cannot visualize how students would fit within the network or what their role would be. Opportunities such as these can and should become part of secondary school experience for many reasons.

In education, acquiring knowledge and techniques and understanding processes is important, but the ability to apply these qualities, in authentic context, ultimately determines and defines success or failure in most settings. Young professionals are routinely required to apply their school learning experiences to new situations early in their careers. We also know that learning does not stop once one leaves the classroom, and usually, continued learning becomes a necessary condition for success within any profession. Where can young people today find context, relevancy, and applications for what they learn in school? The opportunity to do this exists in every community and can become an important part of any secondary school experience. The examples in the first paragraph can become valid within the classroom curriculum. We want our students to have these experiences in safe, well-managed, and supportive environments.

The goal or outcome of reading about our community program is to open the doors to community educational opportunities and partnerships for educators, mentors, and students. These ideas may include traditional community interactions, such as job shadowing, classroom volunteers, and guest speakers, but may also go well beyond these by recruiting mentors—experts within their professions—to help structure unique learning pathways to better serve the needs of the students and teachers in motivating and interesting ways. This model includes students working with authentic problems, whenever possible, that are typical of the problems that mentors solve within their professions. It is hoped that examples and experiences from an existing program can be used to help you design and adopt a new program in your community.

I have included a section specifically for potential mentors. I have found that a document such as this is a very helpful first step in communicating a clear vision of what their role might be. The information in this section can act as a trigger to provide ideas for your own descriptions. You will need to modify it to reflect your needs and vision for the collaborations and partnerships. In addition, samples of current project descriptions and student insurance waivers are included.

The potential for many self-motivating, purposeful, enriching, and relevant educational experiences are in every community, not just in the classroom. Each one of the examples from the first paragraph has the potential to inspire and motivate students. Each one offers opportunities with no real clear guidelines or linear recipes for implementation. However, it is hoped that the information contained within this book can help those interested in education create a new paradigm that incorporates all the resources within one's own community. The tone of the first few chapters is persuasive as well as informative. In following chapters, additional information describes the workings of our mentor program and provides answers to many of the questions that visitors have asked over the years our program has been implemented. Creative educators can make the connections to these opportunities within the community and make them come alive for students.

1

Taking the Classroom
Into the Real World:
One School's Approach

The program and experiences described here were the outcome of the development of a successful interactive community program within a smaller academic "school within a school" at Piner High School. Piner High School, a school of roughly 1,600 "salt of the earth" students, is divided into six smaller self-contained learning communities offering various educational experiences and pedagogy. The school is considered a "restructuring school." Piner High School is affiliated and associated with various restructuring organizations, programs, and models. The school actively seeks and has benefited from grants and other forms of support. Students, with their parents, are able to select the smaller community that most nearly meets their personal educational goals and needs.

The small school community of about 250 students where I and seven other teachers teach is called C-TEC, the Center for Technology, Environment and Communication. The educational areas or specialties that define our smaller school community include our applied use of technology and our ability to embed traditionally taught information, book content, and process into a problem-based context for classroom activities. Teaching in this style is inherently more interesting and motivating for both the teacher and the students than many traditional teaching delivery systems. We (the teachers in C-TEC) often use environmental concerns as a focus or vehicle for activities because of that topic's ability to engage students. Emphasis is placed on the skills and techniques that clearly and effectively communicate ideas, thoughts, and results in authentic, real-world applications. Students gain a new sense of importance for their work because outcomes are shared and critiqued by a wider audience. Examples include:

- A video production on nonpoint pollution, created by our students, which was shown on a local television station
- A student project group that monitored ground water levels and other issues relating to gravel mining on a local river and presented their research findings to the local County Board of Supervisors
- Pamphlets, created and written by students, included in local water bills alerting citizens to water-saving methods and pollution problems

As a teaching staff, we also try to connect the traditional disciplines around thematic units, thus creating opportunities to combine teaching and learning activities that meet a number of individual teaching needs and goals. Our goals are to find the connections and applications between disciplines and apply them in a realistic and relevant context to problems or themes taken from our own community whenever possible. Our restructured courses and their descriptions were some of the first nontraditional courses in the state to receive University of California accreditation as academic courses providing the rigor and content the University of California system requires in college-prep classes. We are perceived by the community and the school as appealing to a more motivated and academic student. This is not totally true. C-TEC appeals to a wide range of abilities and is attractive to students who feel we offer the learning tools and opportunities to learn in a style in which they feel they can be successful. Students usually are free to work in a variety of pedagogical styles, within the school's classes, to meet their needs and maximize their potential for success.

In addition to the above-mentioned areas, we are most noted for our community mentor project work. This is the most visible part of our program and the area that receives the greatest attention and interest. This is the portion of our program that is defined in this book.

Currently, we have about 180 students in year-long project classes. These classes are our main connection to the community and mentors. These classes maximize the potential for learning in off-campus settings and using professionals in many areas. In addition, students can be engaged in working on problems that could not be brought into the classrooms.

For C-TEC students, a project class is a class with a teacher that offers a variety of year-long educational paths for discoveries and explorations within that teacher's expertise. Offerings vary from working at a marine lab or wastewater treatment plant to video production, computer animation, or criminal law. Each year, there are 10 to 15 different project areas from which to choose, but some students find their own mentors and projects. Teachers act as a major resource or coach in creating, planning, implementing, and communicating the students' project work. A richness and relevancy is added as teachers and their students also work with community professionals who mentor students in their projects.

Mentors bring a variety of unique educational opportunities that allow students to work in specialized areas on authentic problems that the mentors bring to or develop with the students. The mentors connect school activities to the real-world relevance outside the classroom. These experiences are driven and motivated by the individual student's or student group's own special interest. Students use a portfolio structure to organize the design, development, implementa-

tion, management, and communication of their experience.
The structure of the portfolio is described in later chapters.

There are many steps to the creation of a successful mentored project. Planning is a collaborative effort. Now, more
than ever, it includes parents and administrators. Projects are
open-ended and usually offer something for all ability, interest,
and motivation levels. Each project may offer opportunities
for an individual, a few, or many students, and usually there
are a variety of opportunities within each area. The following is a sample of the project topics that students are offered:

- We have a working relationship at a University of California marine laboratory and have researcher/teacher
  mentors working with students on many life science
  topics.
- A city engineer included C-TEC in an Environmental
  Protection Agency grant. The grant helped create a
  nonpoint pollution test site at Piner High School. A
  public education component allowed students to design and create a nonpoint TV commercial and water
  bill inserts alerting the public to nonpoint pollution
  problems.
- A gravel mining company that is mining a local river is
  working with students to determine the hydrology of
  the groundwater recharge.
- A chemist from wastewater treatment is working with
  students on sewage contamination on a river by doing
  bacterial studies.
- Video production and animation teams are creating
  original productions and documenting research projects.
- Students in a criminal law project routinely visit the local
  courts to experience and learn about the justice system.

The school has had many visitors and inquiries over the
years about how teachers structure and maintain a successful community program, and they have had many common
questions. The school and community have provided many

successful educational opportunities and experiences for our students. I felt a need to document what we have learned during our project experiences and communicate the basic nature of what we have done. This is not a "how-to" book, but it is a "share" book. My intention is not to expect all teachers to do what we do; we have not created a set formula. All educators, mentors, and students need to know what is possible and build on it. We want high school to be more meaningful and relevant for all teachers and students. Take out of this book what you think could work for you, modify it, use it, and make it your own.

Before beginning our adventure, we will define a few terms.

A *mentor* is a person, not technically a teacher, interested in providing the same things that teachers provide for students. Mentors usually make their living in some profession other than education.

Projects, in the context of this book, are interesting and motivating educational pathways or experiences that are designed and developed by mentors and teachers to impart to students the knowledge and skills necessary to be successful in their careers.

Open-ended refers to educational experiences that have multiple educational opportunities within the same project. A project also may have aspects that appeal to the many ability levels and interests within the same classroom. For example, a group of science students, with an ecologist, may be working on an endangered wetland species census while another group is creating a documentary video to communicate the need to conserve wetlands; a smaller group is engaged in teaching wetland ecology at local elementary schools. This could be within the same class or shared with other classes. In this example, a journalism class prepared brochures that were used as handouts at presentations. The process of learning to complete an authentic task is the focus, not the result. Outcomes in this case could be a scientific paper from one group, a scripted video from another, and the elementary classroom presentations from the third.

Outcomes are project or educational goals and objectives as defined by students' mentors and teachers. These may be very different because each project participant, including the teacher and mentor, have different outcomes in mind within the same project paradigm.

Frustrations include the "hoops" we have to jump through to get to our outcomes. In projects, frustrations give us the opportunity to have students experience, with our guidance and help, what it is really like to try to get "real work" done.

Real world is a phrase that describes our effort to create greater student connections between the skills and knowledge being taught in the classroom and the skills and knowledge required in post-high school experiences.

Content and processes include the more traditional stuff we find in most textbooks; canned labs; and contrived, less authentic (as related to job skills) school activities. I do not view the basics—reading, writing, and math—as contrived, but they are usually taught out of context. However, the applications of these basic skills—the school work to which we have traditionally applied them—may be less relevant and therefore may be seen by students as not being directly important to them.

2

Changing Roles for Teachers

Why change? Simply put, teachers can use the help. Funds are limited, and most teachers are asked to do more with less. In many communities, we can see the power of the public within sports programs. Parents build fields and buy equipment, form huge organizations to facilitate youth sports, and travel endless miles on weekends to and from events. Construction companies donate time. Businesses become sponsors and contribute funds. School sports are big, but community sports organizations are, in many cases, bigger. If the same effort was put into off-campus academic opportunities, everyone would win. As mentors, the working public becomes integrated into the schools and the school becomes integrated into the community. The potential to add to any teacher's or school's resource bank is tremendous.

Secondary school classrooms are asked to meet the educational needs and expectations of students and parents from all segments of the general community in Everytown, U.S.A. Many times, this is difficult within any single classroom. Teachers know that this is difficult because of large class sizes and the wide variety of motivational, interest, and ability levels they deal with in their classrooms. Lessons and classroom activities rarely meet the needs of an entire classroom. Students know this because motivated students often have to tolerate watered down, less challenging lessons; a slow classroom pace; and the behavioral distractions of peers. Colleges and universities know it because many students lack the tools and motivation to be successful in post-high school educational programs.

A strong program of mentored relationships provides teachers with opportunities to address these problems. If a student has a vision of working as a lawyer, doctor, or physical therapist, a long-term mentor in any of these fields could provide a motivational experience that creates a context and relevancy to the classroom curriculum. Such experiences create a purpose for learning and help students set concrete goals, objectives, and pathways for further education. This occurs formally within structured mentored projects and informally as students share their personal experiences.

In addition, secondary schools are asked to prepare students for successful transition to college and/or the world of work. This involves the transfer of current "general knowledge" in a wide number of disciplines and skills in order to do well on a variety of standardized tests. Thinking logically, following directions, and adopting "high-level thinking skills" are critical and are expected to be taught. Also, schools are asked to teach students how to learn, work cooperatively, and set and achieve short- and long-term goals, in addition to meeting students' extracurricular and emotional counseling needs. A mentored program clearly creates pathways and contributes to achieving these goals, in many cases in a much more authentic mode than can be created in a classroom setting. The roles that students assume in schools are, in many cases, different from the behaviors required upon leaving school. A mentor and a mentor program can begin to model and facilitate behaviors that will be required outside the classroom. I have heard it said that school is the last place that students will have to do many of the various activities they are asked to do there.

In most mentored educational projects, this is not the case, because the demands of the project are very real. The types of mentored activities that are presented in this book offer additional educational options that have worked for us. Simply put, we engage more students in meaningful academic performance than we did in the past.

Teachers only have to look to their own experiences in the educational setting. We, as teachers, have had many experiences orchestrated for us that may never need to be used, repeated, or needed in our "real world." We rarely engage mentally in work that does not directly support our own classroom efforts. Generally, teachers want to participate only in workplace activities that support successful classroom or general educational practice.

Like most people who need to learn as a condition of their jobs, we learn best if we have a direct need to know something and can apply it to something important to us. Many students feel the same way and exhibit less patience than do teachers. Teachers are continually looking for interesting lessons that can help motivate students to think and learn, and that will eliminate discipline problems. Boredom and disinterest are the enemy, and we have only a short time frame at the beginning of each semester or year to impress students with our ability to hold their interest. We want students and parents to trust us to provide them with the educational tools they will need.

In summary, mentor programs, as described in this book, offer a wider range of pathways and opportunities for teachers to meet the needs of their students. They are as follows:

- Mentored activities such as these supplement, enhance, and validate existing curricular activities. Once implemented, they can become an integral part of the everyday curriculum.
- Many times, students gain a sense of relevance and context for their school work within the mentored project.
- Mentored project activities are open ended in nature and students have the ability, with the collaboration of the mentor and the teacher, to explore and create their own project pathways and explore their personal interests.

- Abstract ideas about many occupations become concrete for those experiencing a taste of what they view as a potential career.
- Many mentored projects require responsibilities that aid students in role and behavior transitions.
- Longer-term relationships with mentors offer greater immersion and more meaningful experiences than do job shadowing, career days, or guest speakers.
- Mentors become community advocates for education and the school.
- Relationships with businesses, industry, and public agencies can provide resources that the school cannot.
- The mentor program model described here is open ended, which allows many people, businesses, industries, and public agencies to contribute in mutually designed programs within their own comfort zone.
- The community, much like in sports programs, becomes an active, not a passive, participant in your academic program.

Modifying the Teaching Paradigm

To begin, mentored project work takes more work then the organized "chapter march." Project teachers have to be creative, open to people who may know more about their subject than they do, and able to think on their feet as unexpected problems come up. The teacher's role changes from a provider of information to a provider of structure, support, and connections to the resources the mentor and students need. Teachers facilitate and create the vision for the collaboration and the project. Some of the following potential role changes are offered for your consideration.

- Teachers facilitate these mentored relationships. Teachers will need to consider the mentor-to-student or -project ratios. There has to be enough challenge, opportunity, and interest generated to sustain the targeted student group. Some mentors feel comfortable with larger groups, and others will want only a few students. Mentors who participate for a couple of years usually want to focus on a small number of students after the first year. Remember, teachers can act as mentors as well. Most teachers have their own areas of interests, such as music, computer technology, and so on that could be shared with small student groups.

- Teachers orchestrate opportunities for student self-direction. Teachers and mentors can put together loose frameworks for the projects to present to students. Once presented, students can add or modify the frameworks to suit their own interests or add their visions to yours. This serves as a beginning to students taking ownership of the project or projects and needs to be done with each mentored group. One of my mentors, an ecologist from the Bodega Marine Laboratory, encourages students to pick the type of research topics they are interested in doing. Some projects require group efforts, whereas others can be handled by individuals. Some research projects are feasible, and others are beyond the scope of our time and resources. He always has some back-up investigative topic suggestions for those who do not know what they want to do.

- Teachers act to connect community work with more traditional curricula. A personal balance between project work or mentor interaction and other class activities needs to be decided. Teachers strive to enhance and link the concepts and ideas and their application within a mentored problem or project. It is important to work with students and mentors to design and define specific pathways, activities, and tasks within a project to accomplish all of this. C-TEC created a specific projects class for these activities. This is not always necessary; mentor programs can be integrated successfully and can enhance curricula in any discipline or class.

- Teachers need to assess, evaluate, and assign grades for mentored work. Evaluation of this type may call for content assessment, but more important, a process-based or "authentic" assessment model is required to gauge student performance accurately. This may be new to some, and it is addressed in later chapters. If students are doing project work in class one day a week, one fifth of their in-class time is project work. If it is to be considered homework, then some compensation will have to be given. Most students want to know what they have to do to get a good grade. You will need to be prepared to respond to that question with concrete student objectives. Not all students do this, but there will be a few. You may want students working within groups to have specifically defined tasks for which they can be held accountable apart from group goals.

- Teachers, accountable to school protocols, need to set a timetable (usually the school's) for assessment and evaluation. This would include setting a pace for the project, as well as intermediate and final outcomes or demonstrations of mastery or progress, which all agree upon and think reasonable. Most mentors want to work with students rather than handle paperwork. However, many seniors ask their mentors for letters of recommendation. A letter request is generally the outcome of a successful relationship. Some mentors will help with assessment, whereas others will not feel comfortable with it.

- There are times when mentors will need funds for some aspect of the project; teachers may need to consider this and budget whatever funds they have for this. Sometimes, principals have access to special funds. Mentor teachers sometimes have a budget for alternative programs, or gifted and talented education (GATE) funds could be available. Offering monetary support, even if minimal, may sustain a project and make a difference in its quality.

- And finally, teachers will need to rally parent support for the enriching experiences their students are having. Parents do not always remember that mentors are volunteers.

Once preparations are complete, each project or mentored activity develops on its own, and the rewards are great. Students will take ownership of the mentored project. You may no longer be a "stand-and-deliver" teacher. The mentor becomes the content expert. You now have the responsibility to create the paths of exploration the students and mentors will take. Mentors generally do not have an educational background; they are successful at what they do and want to share their experience with your students but do not always know how. You know your students, so place them according to their interests and your perception of which project offers them the greatest chance for success. As with activities within the classroom, balancing a range of student behaviors, interests, and motivation is a big part of any project's success.

Students need paths built and goals created that are reasonable and attainable. Students do not all come with the same toolbox. If they are to work in groups, consider the group dynamics and chemistry. Project topics need to be chosen for their richness, real-world relevancy, and their ability to motivate and interest students with a variety of abilities and needs. They also need to fit into and become part of your curriculum. A mentored project is a collaborative effort, but you are the expert here.

Another benefit that affects the teacher more directly is the teacher/mentor interactions. I look at the time I spend with mentors as inservice time. How many inservices, staff meetings, and committees have you been in or on that allow you to work with people on the cutting edge of your discipline? Teachers rarely have opportunities to interact with colleagues in other schools. We generally work in a very narrow and closed environment. Teachers work with other teachers and rarely are given the opportunity to work with people who need to really apply what we teach. Interactions with mentors keeps our perspective fresh and in touch with the real and applied state of our discipline.

3

Mentoring: New Roles and Learning Outcomes

Authentic work products become the outcomes of mentored curricula. These outcomes may be very different from most curricular outcomes. One of the basics for planning long-term teacher, mentor, and student experiences is setting expected outcomes for the collaborations. The following are examples of student outcomes:

- Gaining the knowledge, technique, and processes necessary to answer a scientific research question by investigation and then writing a paper
- Creating, developing, and applying a multimedia computer program as an educational tool to teach elementary school students on a "Salmon in the Classroom" experience
- Writing and publishing an informational coaching and sports injury manual
- Documenting a research project with video or presenting the results of research to the authentic audience

These products are important outcomes for the students, but teacher and mentor educational outcomes are very different. In many cases, they are not as concrete or as easily identified within the project but may be more important than visible outcomes.

- Our outcomes involve the creation and orchestration of collaborative pathways of self-discovery, exploration, and a rewarding educational experience.

Our agendas are hidden. Mentors assume roles similar to coaches. They are there to prepare students to work within the project, helping with their expertise and experience. Ideally, in most mentored relationships, we want the students' roles to change. We want students to begin to share responsibility and take ownership of whatever problem or project they are working on with their mentors.

- Another hidden goal is a collaborative relationship with the student's personal engagement and buy-in.

Self-motivation, direction, and confidence are the products of a successful relationship. Project participants, rather than the teacher, begin to identify what they need to know and do to complete the project. As students develop more active roles within projects, mentors and teachers will need to do less. It is much like training a new person within any profession.

- We also want to expand the classroom.

Learning can take place anywhere. Students will work off-campus and at research sites on weekends and after school when they are truly involved. In one case, students realized on their own that they needed around-the-clock data on the movement of salamanders in a pool for their study and arranged with parents to spend nights at the site to collect it. Getting a feel for salamander behavior just could not be done during the school day alone. Other students will arrange field trips to unique locations and study sites to supplement their classroom participation. They will find rides to the courthouse for an important hearing. At C-TEC, many students want their classrooms open late afternoons and on weekends to use the technology and equipment in their classrooms on their projects.

- We want students to experience a little of what the mentor's job demands and become immersed in a related problem or project.

To further define the mentoring role, mentors also bring the nature and flavor of their work to the students, not just to tell interested learners about their work but to create opportunities for students to experience the specific career firsthand. Content and process can be embedded carefully in the project experience. Frustrations can be selectively placed and avenues for success created. Student, teacher, and mentor project collaborations should offer experiences rich in content but also rich in opportunities to learn how to get work done in an organized, effective way. In addition, it should offer paths to experience and overcome problems inherent in any project we typically experience in most work sites. This includes modeling solutions to the frustrations we all face at the workplace and helping students build the skills and confidence to deal with and work through these frustrations on the road to a successful project. We are not just telling them what they need to know. We are building a customized program and a structured path within the project that is motivating and interesting and then "coaching" the students on their journey.

4

Looking for Help:
Recruiting Mentors

Finding Mentors

Mentor recruitment is an area that inhibits many teachers who are otherwise interested in doing project work. From our experience, mentors are easy to find. Most people want to help but do not have a clear vision of how to do it without its intruding too far into their time and responsibilities. Careful consideration, thought, and planning can alleviate their concerns. We usually have more prospective mentors than we have time to pursue. The key is flexibility and a willingness to work with what the potential mentors are willing to provide.

As a science teacher, I look into my community to see where the science is being done. I also look into my curriculum to see where mentoring could fit and enhance learning and teaching. Many times, I lack the resources to cover some topics as well as I would like, and a mentor or community source may help. Sometimes, there is just something interesting going on that I want to include, and I target that.

Various scientific businesses and public agencies exist in most cities and towns. Science is being done in most community colleges and universities, as well as in governmental agencies, such as those concerned with water and air quality, fish and game, and forestry. For those in other disciplines, law is being practiced in every aspect of community life. Papers are published and products produced. Research is being done in most college and university disciplines. I had two seniors working as urban archaeologists, going to a local college and sorting through soils collected from an Oakland, California dump in a historic part of town. As part of their work, they were to document the evolution of this study from funding to local politics, in addition to the science. There are museums, courthouses, and public works departments with engineers and city planners. These are good places, both public and private, to look for mentor project activities.

Businesses and public agencies will contribute professionals in the form of donated hours. Sometimes, they will allow the use of technologies and equipment that schools cannot provide. We do not overlook our students' parents, either. As we describe the program during parent nights, interested parents are asked to sign up if they feel they have something to offer. Parents are a primary source of contacts.

We approach all businesses and public agencies the same way. We do not have a set plan for involvement or ask for anything. Once we communicate the nature of the program and provide a range of examples, both sides begin to see the possibilities. Most organizations are willing to work with us because we want their help and cooperation on their terms, and mentors usually end up putting in much more time than they originally felt they could.

The typical process of recruitment is outlined here.

The First Visit

Our project program, with examples, is presented during the first visit to a potential project mentor organization or individual. The first person with whom you speak, in most organizations, may not end up as the mentor. After the initial visit and contact, the person with whom you speak about project work usually shares it with others in the organization or will delegate further discussion to people that might have a greater interest in participating in your program.

The Second Visit

In most cases, this visit brings in the potential mentors. Generally, they are afraid you are going to ask for more than they are willing to provide. Your job is to be "user friendly," find out what they are willing to give or do, and see if it will work for you. We again define the nature of the program, clearly and completely. This includes time commitments and a discussion about what other mentors have done in the past or your personal vision based on your needs. Many people think you want them to come in and present their work or set up job shadow or visitations. Be clear about your vision. Working with students is very different from a simple visitation or presentation. If the discussions go well, they can evolve into more specific planning.

Planning and Design

The next step is to set up another conversation after both sides have had time to reflect on the possibilities. Invite them to your school, share ideas and new possibilities, and discuss limitations. We want mentors to help orchestrate paths of self-discovery within real problems from the students' own community and the mentors' own workplace. Sometimes it will not work, and that is all right—the chemistry is not always there. Experience gives you a better feel for the potential of a relationship. If things have gone well to this point, the relationship can become more concrete, and real planning and collaboration can occur. Now is the time to decide on the details. Start with expected outcomes—what you want your students to know and do at the end of the project. Share these ideas with the mentor, and then create the paths to get there.

The number of mentors with whom you work is up to you. It may take a few to meet your needs. When and where they mentor is up to you. Some project activities occur off-site, whereas others occur at school. Try to have options so that students without transportation can participate.

Liability and Insurance Issues

Insurance and liability problems can be worked out with your school administration and the mentor agency. Additional district liability is scary for administrators, but there are models from athletics and work-experience-type programs that can be examined for precedent. Your district business manager is a good place to start. In our case, our principal set up a meeting with the business manager and district insurance carrier. Once project and student activities were clear, we shared it all with the appropriate district personnel and insurance carrier. We described the activities and eliminated or changed those with which the district was not comfortable. In one case, a mentor wanted students to take samples of a specific species of fish for a population census within a lake, which would require students to go out in boats. We did not do that project, but rocky ocean intertidal research was fine with appropriate preparation. A well-planned presentation, a modeling organization, and control over the activities goes a long way toward putting district administrators at ease. This approach also works with parents.

If students are to work at facilities and sites with mentors outside the school, each mentor's organization may have its own insurance protocols. We had students working at a University of California laboratory and field study site that required its own release and waiver forms to be signed by students and parents.

After these discussions, we design necessary waiver and release forms. Students who participate in sports or work experience programs can provide a model for off-campus activities; find out how teachers handling those programs deal with these issues. Be prepared with answers to administrative, mentor or mentor agency, or parent concerns before they ask. Plan parent meetings with mentors present. Identify the risks up front, work through them, and mitigate or eliminate them. Many administrators will see potential trouble with many activities unless you show them you are on top of the potential problems.

In some cases, you may have a student or parent who is just not comfortable with an activity, and you will have to have options available. In our school, off-campus projects can be only an option, and we have to have on-campus alternatives. Laboratory work, maintenance of collected plants and animals, computer programming, multimedia or literary production, and many other project-related activities can be done at school. In some cases, half of a group may work off campus and half on campus.

What About Credentialing and Supervision?

Where do we look to begin to define a noncredentialed mentor's, student's, or teacher's role within a community program? The ultimate responsibility for the nature of any student's experience falls on the teachers, parents, and the school administration. Each project, mentor, or student group needs to be considered individually. Ultimately, each school, student, mentor, and community entity will need to explore and define its own comfort zone within any educational activity. Because we offer many opportunities and options for project work both on and off campus, parents and students can be full participants without exceeding limits of personal comfort zones. This also works for mentors. Many business and agencies would rather not have students in their workplaces but will work with students at school or other field sites.

There are many examples of programs that use noncredentialed people in educational settings. In many high school athletic programs, noncredentialed community members act as coaches who assume full responsibility for student athletes and sports teams. This includes off-campus travel, practices, matches, and games. Occasionally, some coaches with appropriate licenses do drive athletes. As fewer teachers participate in extracurricular activities, the need for noncredentialed coaches and supervisors increases. Parents of athletes routinely sign releases and permission documents as a condition of participation.

Work experience programs have been a part of schools for years. Students leave campus to work in off-campus settings, much like our students leave campus to work on a specific project. Parents are involved because they either provide transportation or permit the student to drive him- or herself to and from school and work before, during, and after school hours. Like parents of athletes, parents of students in mentor programs sign releases and permission documents. While students are at work, usually no teachers are present, and supervision is the responsibility of the manager of the business, who may or may not be present. Liability issues may fall on the participating business or the parents as a condition of participation.

Finally, many teachers or instructional aides take on teaching roles under the direct or indirect supervision of teachers and administrators. Interaction with students may occur anywhere on campus, and roles sometimes blur. Library and computer room aides often take on responsibilities much like those of teachers.

If programs like these already exist within a school district, it would be hard to argue against a mentor or other type of academic community learning program. Credentialed school personnel do not always directly supervise students but do create and supervise student programs.

As far as working within a teacher's credentialed area, most teachers create mentored programs that reflect the needs of students within their specific disciplines. Communication is again essential. When parents and administrators are familiar with the workings of a program, many problems or misunderstandings are avoided.

In closing, flexibility is the key here. Project opportunities usually end up as a compromise between your needs or vision and what the mentor or his or her agency will provide. There is no set formula for recruitment of mentors or the creation of a project except for keeping an open mind for opportunities for your students. Working with individuals who use what you teach in their jobs keeps you fresh, current, and aware of the skills and abilities that are required in the real world. Sometimes we forget what we, as students, thought was important and motivating in our school experience. When you think back to when you were in school and about those few memorable activities, what really was important to you? Rarely was it a chapter in a book. Mentors and mentored projects can stand out from the day-to-day curriculum and make a real difference in a student's life and how he or she views the community.

5

Communicating With the Community and the Mentors

In actual practice, communicating the community education vision is not always easy. The following approach has worked. The idea is to not only allow participants to work within a teacher's or school's vision for involvement but to also engage them in the creation and design of it. If I were creating a pamphlet or handout that describes the program, it might look something like the following:

> We want your help and invite you to explore, with teachers, potential ways to provide educational experiences to our students beyond the classroom. We are offering you the opportunity and structure to share what you do with students interested in your field. When the community becomes the school, everyone wins. What if the community got behind academic opportunities the way it gets behind community and school sports? Usually, whole communities get behind extracurricular activities. We all know learning does not begin or end at the classroom door. Most of us learned what we really needed to know once we got into our jobs. Schools gave us the basics and sometimes the interest and motivation to continue into

an occupation of our choice. If we were lucky, we had a few people in our lives who believed in us and helped create and support our dreams. Anyone can fill that role, not just teachers.

Acting as a mentor or providing a project has the potential for having a major positive impact on our students. Professionals know, usually better than our teachers, what it takes to be a scientist, writer, computer programmer, or video producer. Many businesses and public agencies play a role in shaping and defining the identity of a community by sponsoring sports teams and participating in civic organizations. A community is defined by the quality and caring of its residents.

We, as teachers, want to bring the community into the schools in new ways. Mentors and long-term connections and relationships during collaborative projects unify our community's educational efforts. We want mentors to know what we do, know our students, and know our problems. Together, we create avenues to solutions. We cannot teach unmotivated and disinterested students. Mentors and long-term projects connect students to the realities of the workplace and the knowledge and skills they require. You make our curriculum relevant and alive. Collaborations with mentors create a more authentic environment for experimentation, exploration, and learning that beats a "chapter march" and worksheets every time.

There are many levels on which community agencies, businesses, and professionals can contribute. You can contribute to local schools in ways that will be rewarding for you without interfering with your business or job activities, and in some cases will provide you with tangible benefits. We hope you will consider participation and collaboration with teachers, which can begin to inspire creative possibilities that can work for everyone, most importantly for students.

What We Are Looking For:
Educational Methodologies for Mentors

We want you to help us build opportunities for students to apply what they learn and experience in the classroom. Creating a safe and structured environment supports a high potential for a successful experience. This section should give you an idea of how we do it. We recognize that a mentor program can be an integral part of a student's classroom or school experience. We also recognize that many mentors, although experts in their own fields, could be uneasy about working with teachers and students. Mentored relationships are very unique and may include curriculum and teaching methods you may not have experienced. We hope that we can give you a brief idea or recipe for overcoming any reluctance or concerns you have. We want to help structure and implement the project with the greatest chance for student success and provide a rewarding experience for you as well. Things you can count on:

1. Teacher support in managing and structuring the project, student accountability, parental involvement, and evaluation and final communication of the work

2. Collaboration on your timetable

3. Parental support, at least for transportation, and sometimes more help

4. Open-ended opportunities in structuring your project on and off campus

There is no minimum or maximum time commitment. Your relationship and contribution are open ended. We have mentors who communicate with students via e-mail or telephone only, and we have mentors who visit the school or have students go to their work site. The nature of the project interaction and communication is very flexible.

The idea, in this type of educational experience, is to foster a collaborative relationship where students take some responsibility in choosing an area that interests them, and the mentor helps by selecting problems, experiences, and projects from the real world. The collaboration then plans, structures, implements, modifies, and communicates the outcomes of the work. Roles for teachers and mentors are defined. The work can be original, or you may know the outcomes, but the students do not need to know that. Teachers want the students to feel that their work is important to you, and we want them to take "ownership" and have it become theirs. Ideally, we are orchestrating and building paths of exploration and self-discovery and adding a little mystery for motivation. We want to avoid the "canned labs," lectures, and worksheets and instead model how work gets done in your workplace. If we construct our activities well enough, traditional content and process will be needed to solve a project step or problem; thus, the project activity fosters and motivates the students' need to know. Then, at this point, we teach and coach. Knowledge and technique become important tools to solve interesting and motivating problems. It becomes much easier to teach when students want to know and want to apply what they know.

In addition to this, we also want to integrate and connect the curriculum from all the major school disciplines. We recognize that most things taught in isolation really work together everywhere else but in school. Please have high expectations for student communication, math, and other skills required in the project. Students may need to be taught the proper protocols appropriate to your area. Also, feel free to help students understand some of the moral or ethical questions that may apply to their project.

Planning sessions with all involved—students, parents, mentors, and teachers—help all participants to come to common understandings about the nature of the experience. This is an opportunity to define your expectations, identify risks, or cover other areas of concern. We try to limit the misunderstandings and problems before they begin. Parents do not remember school being like this. It is new to them. Teachers will explain to them that we want to simulate real job-site skills, collaboration, cooperation, deadlines, resourcefulness, and so on. This helps them begin to understand our major goals. Students are not used to taking so much responsibility for their own learning, and parents no longer just drop their students off at school. It is a new way of learning and teaching in an old system, and we need them to buy in. They have to be taught to learn like this. Most of us learn on the job and rarely return to a classroom setting after completing school. The way we, as professionals, learn on the job is similar to the way we want our students to learn.

6

Is There Room
for Something New?

Planning for projects, a problem-based and theme-based pedagogy, is an ongoing activity for us. We see education as a process (teaching students how to learn) as well as a body of knowledge. We do have mentors work with classes, but it is more typical to have mentors working with our students in their projects class. The projects class is an elective that allows a student to work on problems or programs of their choice, usually with a mentor and sometimes off campus. They may work at a local lab, field study site, or other community location based on the nature of their project focus. This is something like a work experience model, except that it is more academically focused. The class itself gives a student credit in the discipline that most clearly fits the student's project activity and level of complexity. The closest model that fits or looks like our project model is an independent study or special project class in a college or university setting.

The projects class works for us, but we do not envision a projects class in every school. However, the "project idea" could become a big part of a more traditional class. Usually, the first argument or concern that comes up from teachers is "I already have too much to teach," and I agree. Even when

I taught in a more traditional way, I could not cover it all. I covered what I was more successful at teaching or what I knew best. Giving up chapters became easier as I worked to embed the content in the project experience. A carefully constructed project will drive the need to know the content. That allows me to cover those lessons that did not lend themselves to the project's context.

Again, this is where teachers who are new to this teaching style have trouble. They feel that they, and sometimes the parents feel that students, miss out on important material. It is my feeling that students remember and retain curricula in which they are sincerely engaged. What did you remember from your high school experience? What activities prepared you best for college or your profession? Our goals are knowledge, content, and sometimes process, but the most important goal we have is to create enthusiasm, motivation, and interest. These intangibles will carry students further than hitting every chapter in the book. I am not advocating doing away with more traditional teaching, but I think we need to look at what is really valuable and important to students' future success for the long term and find a balance. Is it sometimes harder to teach this way? Yes it is, but it is much more rewarding.

Curricular Accountability

Problem-based learning within projects, like any other teaching and learning methodology or instructional strategy, comes under scrutiny from a variety of perspectives. All groups and individuals within educational communities, from students and teachers to parents and administrators, have their own scale for assessing and evaluating the validity of teaching and learning. This is done both informally and formally. Curriculum designers need to be able to justify and provide evidence of the suitability of curricular activities. If teachers are not creating their own curricula, they are bringing it in from other sources. Whether it is produced on site or brought in, it needs to be evaluated for validity. Curricular accountability is at the heart of any validity and effectiveness scale where teaching and learning take place.

What I have done here is provide an example of how a specific problem might be examined for embedded content and process. In addition, I have looked at some of the general features of the problem-based pedagogy unrelated to content and process. These features are important management considerations when assessing the appropriateness of any curricular paradigm.

Content and Process Features

As described in the introduction, there are many standards, frameworks, college and university expectations, guidelines and philosophies, and testing and assessment instruments that address what should be taught in courses and measure what students retain. Some focus on specific vocabulary and content, whereas others focus on concepts and principles, and some include application of content. Few define or assess and evaluate pedagogical effectiveness. Instruments to assess pedagogy can be designed and implemented by teachers. Terms and phrases such as "more is less," "depth not breadth," and "hands on or minds on" add further to curricular confusion. I have seen some very bad "hands-on" activities that were, at best, very loosely related to any scientific principle.

Accountability to content, vocabulary, techniques, and processes may be important in some settings. Although teachers rarely are able to cover all of the content in textbooks, most teachers have specific content areas that they deem very important. The table of contents in textbooks makes it easy to assess coverage. Problem-based learning modules make it a little more difficult. Accountability to the coverage of important curricular content objectives can help justify a change in teaching style, pedagogy, or instructional methodology. A few years ago, a book company, as part of their sales packet, included what they called a "CAP map." This was in California, and CAP meant California Assessment Program. The book publishers wanted to connect their textbook to the performance expectations and content of the state testing. They wanted to show curricular accountability to the test.

Each one of the investigative project examples in this book has a large number of possible pathways, each with its own specific subject or concept emphasis. As you read through them, most paths, themes, and topics are obvious. However, there always seem to be a few students who see a pathway you have not thought of and want to explore it. The beauty of these problems is that modifications and adjustments can be made easily. There are many different spins that can be placed on the same problem, depending on the content and process coverage the teacher desires.

A curriculum writer can connect problem-based activities to concept and process expectations and coverage. Consider the following mentored project experience. It was introduced orally to the class and structured collaboratively on the chalkboard. Because I am a science teacher, I have used a science example. It is hoped that educators from other disciplines can see the potential here.

Algae Blooms in the Laguna de Santa Rosa

A local senior biologist working for a state water agency brought us an environmental problem loaded with chemistry. Much of his job is assessing water quality or other water issues. Over the years, he has been working locally and has followed the yearly summer algae blooms—large algae mats sitting on top of the water in local creeks in the Laguna de Santa Rosa. Historically, these blooms did not occur until recent times. With grazing cattle and agriculture as the primary land use adjacent to the creeks, it is suspected that nutrient chemicals from animal waste and fertilizers wash into the creek during storm events, supporting the heavy growth of algae in nonmoving pools during the warm summer months. The algae alters the habitat by robbing the water of oxygen as it decomposes. Native organisms are affected.

Currently, there is no data or understanding of either the amounts of chemicals in the water and sediments of the creek or how much is retained in the sediments every year. Are the chemicals that are retained in the sediments leaching out during the warm summer months? What are the amounts of nutrient chemicals in the sediments? How much of the nutrient chemicals that wash into the creeks gets into the sediments, and how does water temperature affect the movement of nutrients from water to sediments or sediments to water?

This problem could be addressed with a small group of students or within a chemistry class applying book content and concepts to a real problem. In this case, the agency provided laboratory equipment necessary to do the analysis. All of the chemical processes in this problem related to specific content within most chemistry textbooks. Solvents and solutes, chemical reactions, heat and related chemical behaviors, and so on, in addition to the scientific method and the processes of doing real science, all fall within textbook chapters. Experimental design and constructing valid and reliable methods were all part of this problem. Collection sites were located and samples taken. The rest became laboratory analysis of sediments and water.

The nice part of this project is that it can be repeated year after year and the data compared to previous years. It is quantitative and requires mathematical data analysis, spreadsheets, and the summarized graphing of results. This study could be dissected and matched to any framework or curricular expectations.

The study also has a social and political side in that the results could affect land use. The farmers and ranchers may be required to alter or change their use of the land to protect the watershed. The problem brings the textbook to life.

Groups can work on different study sites or replicate controls to have as many students as possible involved and engaged. Every student can have an important role. The textbook becomes a reference, and students will need to decide what they need to know to answer the questions. There are no right answers here. The results are only as reliable as the methods the students use. Creating the study itself becomes a challenge as the teacher's and mentor's roles become that of coach.

Summary of the Content and Process Features and Characteristics of Problem-Based Project Activities Within the Example

1. Important science concepts, content, and processes can be covered in depth and in context to their application. These are linked together in an integrated and interdisciplinary style.
2. Most problem-based science activities, including the examples, can be linked to a math curriculum in a quantitative, applied, authentic context.
3. Theories and hypotheses can be examined and tested and moral ethical issues can be built in for consideration and examination.
4. Learning opportunities are open ended, not just recipes to right answers, and students are free to explore and experiment within their own interest or learning styles.
5. Laboratory and field work can be integrated within the curriculum.
6. Problems can be designed and developed to use the range of technology and laboratory equipment available at the site. Many "canned" activities are limited by lack of equipment.

Summary of the General Curricular Features and Characteristics of Problem-Based Activities

1. Teachers are free to build cooperative learning opportunities and offer leadership roles within problems. Multiple instructional strategies can be included within the same problem, and mastery can be defined in a number of ways.

2. Special student populations benefit because teachers can customize their opportunities, expectations, and roles within each problem. There is no one right way to learn here.

3. Flexibility is a key attribute of this teaching and learning style. Most problems can be modified and adapted while in process.

4. An appropriate balance between teacher direction and self-direction can be built into problems as the student's experience dictates.

5. Various technologies, ranging from computer programs such as word processors or spreadsheets to traditional laboratory equipment, can be included that enhance and complement the professional atmosphere that teachers want to foster. A portfolio-based management scheme helps assess and provide evidence of a student's effort and accomplishment. Portfolios will be discussed in the next two chapters.

7

Managing It All:
The Portfolio

The entire year-long project experience is structured and held together using an instrument or organizational structure called a portfolio. It is a device that gives the project work structure, form, and built-in accountability. The portfolio itself may be just a file folder filled with information about a student's project work, or it could be something more. Each teacher will have his or her own requirements. The portfolio is the way a student communicates to mentors and teachers. It documents the "process" of doing successful project work. Most professional people are good at structuring their work duties and become very efficient at getting the most out of their efforts, talent, and time. People who have these skills generally are more successful than those who do not. The portfolio becomes the student's working directions, guide, timetable, record, and the hard evidence that work was done. A portfolio in our context is a self-built structure of guidelines and directions for getting things done in an orderly and logical fashion. Project structure and content is guided, designed, developed, and modified in collaboration with mentors and teachers. It provides a process of setting short- and long-term goals and objectives. This helps keep students on track so that they do not get "lost." How we get project work done has to be taught, learned, and practiced. Although we see the final product, it is the planning, efficiency, adjustments, and modifications that a student has experienced during the process of his or her work that develops character, confidence, and good work habits, which ultimately may be more important than the end result. This experience is just as important to us as the finished outcome.

All of this puts students in control of their own investigations, research, and learning experience. The portfolio also provides mentors and teachers with student accountability for evaluation and assessment. Students are responsible for communicating, through their portfolio, mastery of the process and content of their work. In addition to doing the work, they need to successfully communicate it. You can balance and weight the importance of each area of the portfolio with points. You can set intermediate check points or grading requirements. Students with fewer organizational skills need more checkpoints, opportunities for feedback, reinforcement, and points of accountability. Together with the students, build them in. Grading can take place at carefully embedded points during appropriate times throughout the year.

Portfolio structure, major due dates, rigorous expectations, and assessment timetables are similar and standardized throughout our program. The structure of the portfolio is separated into three large sections. The major areas are Design and Development, Implementation, and Communication. Each section has its own timetable, requirements, and evaluation or assessment points created collaboratively. This major structure works well for most disciplines and projects.

The requirements may differ because each teacher may have different needs, intermediate structures, or other requirements. I assign point values to the major areas and then weight intermediate tasks with points within the specific areas. Everything the student completes becomes evidence of a mastery and understanding of the planned project outcomes and a relic in their portfolio.

I have included a number of examples of typical project groups and their portfolio development in the next chapter.

Design and Development

This portfolio section could be considered the most important portion of the project experience. We are composing a shared educational vision between the teacher, mentor, and student that has appropriate scope and rigor and is also "doable" with a reasonable chance for success. You can eliminate many potential problems, have greater peace of mind, and maximize the potential for project success by thoroughly thinking out and planning the project. Design and development ("D and D") has the following three parts summarized here:

- *Introduction.* This part introduces the student's vision of the project and acts as a job description and a projection of how the project is expected to go.
- *Methods and Procedures.* This is the recipe for doing the work and uses "best guess," specific step-by-step plans for the semester. If you could do the project from the student's methods and procedures with minimal confusion or questions, then he or she is on the right track.
- *Timetable.* The timetable is created by the individual student or student group and the collaboration team. It should reflect due dates and project products that they expect to produce or complete by those dates, and it clearly defines when you expect results.

The focus of the design and development is to create and communicate the vision, analyze it, modify it, and agree on it. The collaborative team—the student, mentor, and teacher—usually present the vision to the class for peer review. Once a vision is agreed upon as "doable," we design methods, procedures, and a "best guess" timetable for implementation. If you have students working in groups, I suggest doing a group "D and D" and creating individual "D and Ds" for their roles within the larger groups. Separate roles and visions allow students to be evaluated on the merit of their own work. Separate accountability encourages individual buy-in and responsibility. This is a large amount of work, but it will pay off later. A student's project design and development is communicated by completing an investigation introduction, methods and procedures, and a "best guess" timetable within the teacher's evaluation requirements and the school schedule. The students are given and asked to use the following guidelines.

Introduction

The introduction needs to contain a vision statement that defines the question students are trying to answer, what inspired the question, and why it is important to answer it. In some cases, it will not be a question they are answering; it will be a product they will produce that requires a statement of purpose that defines the overall goals of the project. If you add a paper research component, you may ask students to describe the existing state of knowledge about the subject or question. Students will also need to describe the objectives and goals of the project and make some prediction about their expected outcomes. They also may need to describe why their work is important. If they are doing group work, both the group and individuals need to complete the design and development. Individuals within groups do better with separate, well-defined methods and expected outcomes. The number of students in a project is based on the complexity, richness, and rigor of the project. Individuals need to have equally important roles within the larger group.

Methods and Procedures

Procedures and methods are a recipe or direction for doing an investigation or completing the activities within the project. What students write now is a best guess for methods and procedures needed for the completion of the project. It is a working document and can be changed and adjusted as needed. It is a "what I am going to do" and "how I am going to do it" statement.

Methods are usually designs and paths for gathering information, data, or preliminary work needed for the project. They describe the road and tasks needed to reach the project outcome. Identifying outside-of-school contacts, locating resources, setting up appointments, and requesting information may be some of the things that students will need to put in their methods.

Teachers need to clearly define the difference between "what" students are going to do and "how" they are going to do it. Thinking about the "how" moves planning from the abstract or conceptual to the concrete. An example of a "what" statement might be, "We will collect water samples from the river and test them." This does not tell the reader how they will do it. Correct "how" statements would describe where they were collecting and how the sites were picked, how samples will be taken, what is to be tested, and the procedures for testing. Procedures could include sterile sampling protocols, depth of sampling, date and weather conditions, or length of time before testing the water. To be completed correctly, the directions should be able to be understood and repeated by another project student.

Methods and procedures include other skills or equipment the student may need to have or master to move toward completion of a larger goal. If a student needs to learn a computer program before producing a brochure or video production, that intermediate task needs to go into the methods and timetable. If a student needs to pick 100 students for a survey, a description of how he or she is going to pick the group and create a standard system for data collection needs to be included. Learning techniques and building story boards and flow charts may be appropriate.

Sources of background information, transportation requirements, and evidence for accountability need to be considered by the teachers and students. The most important aspect is the authenticity of the procedures and methods. If students are not really engaged and thinking, they sometimes focus more on "what" they are going to do than "how" they are going to do it. Methods need to reflect *concrete steps* to completing necessary tasks within the project.

Timetable

Communication of the timetable for completion of the project is important for setting realistic goals and meeting the teacher's grading obligations. Setting dates for completing intermediate tasks is very important. Each date can end one step and begin another. It helps if students have defined something concrete to produce. Students need to build their timetables around a school calendar. Due dates need to be made with ample lead time for teachers and mentors to evaluate and grade completed work. We ask for 8 to 16 hours per month of student time outside of class. Completed work usually provides evidence of how much time was spent on the project but a weekly oral report, time log, or journal sometimes works.

The timetable, depending on the maturity of the students, could also include due dates for rough drafts, progress reports, or other intermediate steps. Good design and development should signal the beginning of implementation. My personal evaluation guidelines for Design and Development are as follows.

"A" work is completely ready for implementation with only minor changes to methods, procedures, or timetable. The skills and equipment required by the project can be mastered and acquired by the student. Experimental design, tasks, or outcomes are logical and realistic. Preliminary and intermediate tasks or goals are well defined. Mechanics, format, and grammar contain few errors. The student has engaged in and taken ownership of and responsibility for his or her project.

"B" work may contain errors in methodology. The procedures or timetable require slight modification. The skills and equipment required by the project can be mastered and acquired by the student. Experimental design, tasks, and outcomes are logical and realistic. With modifications, the preliminary and intermediate tasks or goals are well defined. Mechanics, format, and grammar contain few errors. The student has engaged in and taken responsibility for and ownership of his or her project.

Anything less than "A" or "B" work is returned for re-working. An incomplete is given, and the student is allowed a certain amount of time to complete the design and development. If it is not completed within a certain time frame, an "F" grade is given.

Each student is expected to be especially proactive during the creative design and development phase. Students may require a different level of mentor or teacher involvement or "coaching" at this point to work through the rough spots. I call this period "creative confusion." Frustration is part of the experience. Expect students to need solutions to problems. It helps to prethink expected problems and have backup plans ready when students need them. A little help at the right time can act as "glue" in the collaborative bond. Too much frustration can be discouraging and counterproductive.

Implementation

Now is the time to put the conceptual design and development plan into action. The conceptual ideas in the design and development are implemented, tested, refined, or modified. Time on task is important. A student's timetable for preliminary and intermediate steps structures their accountability. What they do is more important than what they say. The phrase "talk is cheap" applies now. You want real products produced and evidence of completed work. Rough drafts, data, and evidence of learned skills are all concrete evidence.

Completion of the design and development sometimes brings a let-down as you start to focus on implementation. We call this let-down an "implementation gulch." It is important to establish a work rate that will lead to the desired outcomes. The more work students do now increases the time available when later, unexpected setbacks arise.

The design plan does not always work, and you may have to cut deals, extend due dates, or otherwise modify the schedule. Expect these changes, and work with the students. I like to assume the coworker role during implementation. I want it to be their work, not mine. They are not doing it for me but for themselves. The definition is subtle. When to be flexible or firm is a matter of practice and being familiar with your students.

Evaluation and grading are based on the quantity of intermediate outcomes and the student's ability to meet the timetable's deadlines. Sign off on their timetable tasks or offer points for the completed tasks at this time.

Communication

The communication portion completes and concludes the project. During this period, a student continues work to complete the project and develops a plan to communicate, in a mode appropriate to the project, the successful outcomes of his or her work. This could include a written scientific paper, seminar, oral presentation, or completed video. It could also include a formal authentic presentation to a community group, board of directors or supervisors, or other community or business organization. In some cases, a speech contest, science fair, or other student competition might be appropriate. You can collaborate on the desired outcome and develop a rubric for evaluation if needed. Including these types of project communications means that the project outcomes will be shared with others besides the teacher or the class. This adds a level of pressure to produce higher-quality work. We have what we call "C-TEC's Night Out." Schedules are created, rooms prepared, and invitations sent to parents, mentors, administrators, and anyone else who has shown an interest in project work during the year. Regard-less of other avenues of project communication, all C-TECers participate in this night. All projects are presented, and this night has become one of the highlights of the year.

Communication completes the student portfolio. Its content depends on the specific project. Individual portfolio pieces become relics supporting growth, understanding, and mastery of the overall project process.

8

Putting the Portfolio to Work: Examples of Student Project Portfolio Evolution

A Typical Project Group

The following is an example of a typical mentored project group and a summary of the project group's portfolio evolution. Within this group, four of the students produced a successful year-long experience, whereas two students had problems.

Two 11th-grade female athletes signed up, along with a group of four 10th-grade male athletes, for a sports medicine and physiology project. It was to be mentored by a local sports rehabilitation and therapy business. The group knew they wanted to work in this area, but none had any concrete ideas. This project was to be research based, with students trying to answer specific questions through investigation. All had 2 weeks or 10 class hours to produce a design that would be ready to implement as a full-blown project. After a few discussions, the two girls decided to research the nature of the word "fit" as it applies to athletes. The question "Are the best athletes the most fit athletes?" made up the key to further project development. How would they answer the question?

After a period of "creative confusion," they concluded that fitness could be broken down into specific categories: cardiovascular efficiency, strength, flexibility, and speed or reaction time. They proposed conducting tests in these areas, with a volunteer study group, to gauge if the "most fit" athletes were the best performers in sports. Their design and development reflected the methods, tests, and experimental designs they would use to answer their question. The cardiovascular test evolved into a basic stress test done on a stair-stepping machine while monitoring blood pressure and pulse rate at various intensities and times. Strength testing involved lifting moderate weights for repetitions and correlating the results to body weight. Reaction times were measured on a simple reaction-timer device, and flexibility was measured in a few standardized stretches. After practicing and revising their methods, the students completed their design and development requirements and implemented their project. The first semester's study group was made up of females. The students ran the tests, collected and organized data, and learned about spreadsheets and graphs. By the end of the semester, they had summarized their results and presented their findings.

The second semester was a repeat of the first, except that males were tested. The mentors helped the students through the process and provided the testing equipment and facilities to do the tests. Their progress was monitored by collecting their data, interviewing them, and having them turn in written summaries of their activities when assessment was required during the school's grading periods. They presented their project to a group of district coaches and at our annual seminar presentations.

Their methods and procedures for collecting project data became the design and development. The testing, data collection, and data manipulation became their implementation. The presentation and seminar became the communication section of their work. All of the documentation that they produced became their personal portfolio and evidence of their mastery of the process. This project went well. We asked these students (and all project students) to develop an individual portfolio. Some teachers may consider a group portfolio as appropriate.

Everything they produced was authentic, relevant, and led to the completion of their project. If there had been flaws or if something was not workable, it would have been returned. If it was to be considered for assessment and had problems, it would have been returned for reworking. An incomplete would be given until acceptable work was completed. "Busy" work, just to get through the grading period, is not acceptable. Authenticity is the key.

Design and Development

The 11th-graders' question drove the need to create methods, procedures, and a timetable to collect the data they would need to answer their question. The itemized methods and the general project design were authentic, detailed, and clearly written to communicate the project planning. Each test required planning, piloting, and adjustments. The students needed to learn the skills that were required to collect data. Their high degree of planning in the design stage demonstrated a clear understanding of the work that needed to be completed in the implementation phase of the project to produce a high probability for a successful project.

Some students may present minimal plans, with holes in procedures or methods. There may be too many unknowns, or you may know they are going to have problems once they begin implementation. I have put off requiring final designs because I know they will have to be modified later. I ask for a preliminary document and expect them to modify and finalize it once they implement and find out which methods or procedures work best. Your experience lets you see the problems that they cannot. Accepting their design and development with flaws in methodologies may not always be bad; the process of working through problems is valuable. Maybe a pass-fail system would work here. A timetable for when they expect to complete tasks is important for account-ability. If they are not ready to really "do" the project, the design and development phase is not complete or needs to be reworked.

Implementation

The data, results, and weekly summaries of progress provided evidence of progress and continued engagement. One teacher required "Learning Logs" weekly, with students discussing specific aspects of the project such as what they had done, what their problems were, and any request for additional help. These were shared with mentors.

Communication

A video of their presentation and seminar along with a formal scientific paper became evidence of their mastery and the products of their project. Other students present to authentic audiences outside of school or demonstrate the application of their computer programs or multimedia presentations. Others enter competitions of one sort or another.

Moving on to the other group members, the first pair of 10th-grade males settled on the following question: Which type of playing field surface produces the greatest number of injuries in professional football? This is not a new question, and there is research in this area, but it was new to the students. They found an Internet Web Site that itemized the National Football League's injury reports every week. Their idea was to look at the individual team's injuries, where teams played last, and quantify the injuries and their severity over the season. The pair did not have to design methods to generate their own data because it already existed, but they did have to be able to organize it and find the patterns within it to answer their question. In addition, they had to produce a design and development plan to reflect how the data were to be analyzed and summarized and who was going to be responsible for what tasks. This was only a semester's project, during the NFL season, but I felt it could lead into a second semester project later. Again, they learned about spreadsheets and graphs. The patterns within the data did not show easily, but they were able to complete the project. The accountability and project progression was similar to the 11th-graders' project.

The complexity and rigor of the second investigation was not as great as the first. However, the second project was appropriate for the students' interest and motivational levels. The 11th-graders had done a project the year before and knew the process, whereas the second group was new to project work.

The second pair of 10th-grade boys wanted to look at the various methods for track sprint training and compare the effectiveness of three programs. This would mean researching a number of existing training programs, selecting or creating their three programs for testing, finding athletes willing to participate, and finding ways to measure their progress. They did complete a design and development plan, but the potential for project success was low. The mentors helped, but they could only do so much. We could see that this plan had many potential problems, but some students are able to adapt and adjust as necessary to work through them. That is part of the experience, yet it should not lead to total discouragement.

Even after discussions about potential problems, they wanted to proceed with the project rather than create a new one. The due dates for the design and development plan were coming up, and changing projects would have required more work. However, finding a sample study group was difficult because 10th-grade males did not have the respect of older male athletes. The project further broke down when the individuals who did participate missed training or varied their training from the original plan. Motivation and effort were hard to quantify, as were the data, which tended not to be reliable. The project broke down as frustration set in.

In this case, either the teacher or the mentor would need to have a back-up plan for the students. It could mean salvaging some aspect of the original idea or brainstorming other ideas. Sticking with a risky plan got them through the design and development phase and a couple of assessment periods, but without major adjustments, the plan was going to break down. Sometimes, students are discouraged, and it becomes hard to motivate them with a new project. After a few project experiences, teachers can begin to define risky projects at the design and development stage and guide students to more appropriate ones. It comes down to this: Some students will become self-sustaining and engaged and will take ownership of their work. This is exciting for mentors and teachers. But others will still look to you to provide them with most of the elements of a project. Becoming self-sustaining, creative, and adaptable can be taught, and working through these types of projects provides a good place for students to learn these traits.

Project Groups in Other Disciplines

We have found the portfolio to be a dynamic learning and management tool. Teachers of disciplines other than science within our program modify the portfolio and its major components to meet their needs. Design and development is nothing more than creating a authentic working plan and timetable for the way a student sees his or her project progressing toward an outcome over a semester. In a criminal law project, designed by a government and history instructor, students visit the courthouse to watch trials. They take notes, complete weekly activity sheets, share experiences, and analyze strategies in preparation for mock trial competitions within and outside the school. Court visitation days make up the timetable, and all the products of their visitations, whatever is agreed upon, are expected to be in the portfolio at the end of a grading period. The road of their participation becomes their portfolio and evidence of individual mastery of the learning process. Computer programmers and multimedia or communication groups keep an individual portfolio much like the science groups. The project process is similar.

As time has passed, all the teachers in our program have settled on similar due dates, portfolio expectations, and work production. We want to standardize the rigor and general goals of the project experience. Individual teachers put their own spin on the wording and the specifics of the portfolio, but the essence of the project portfolio process remains the same for all.

9

Examples of Mentored Project Experiences

You may detect a bias in the following examples. Most of them are from my experiences and lean toward a science content area. We do have project examples from the humanities, mathematics, and English, but I would not be able to provide the firsthand details. However, many of the projects overlap these arbitrary discipline boundaries because the projects are rich enough in other content areas to require skills and provide challenges in these other areas.

Consider the following passage from a letter in *The Bodega Bay Navigator*, March 10, 1994. Jim Sullivan critiques an article from another paper, the *Independent*, on the local feral cat controversy.

> The meanest moment in the article is the gratuitous hatchet job on the Bodega Marine Lab's Drs. Peter Connors and Victor Chow. Not only did Jeff [original author] fail to comprehend that these two full-time professional biologists are in possession of a sophisticated understanding of the subject, but in his zeal to discredit them

he also ridiculed the exemplary work done by the Piner High School science students who executed the field studies. On top of that, the Independent's fearless journalist entirely missed another really interesting success story, Dr. Chow's mentorship of what I'm told is a really great high school science program at Piner. (p. 7)

Although not all of our projects become public controversies, this typifies the kind of experiences we hope students will have. We value the authentic audience.

The letter's impact can be evaluated in a number of ways. First, the students and their mentor created this study. It is obvious that the research had an impact on the writers of both articles. Second, it validates the students' work as important to people other than just the students' teacher. Third, the project and lessons became real-world stuff open to public scrutiny. It was scientific research with a political and emotional side. Although the research was not at a publishable level, it was authentic and began to answer some questions about feral cat behavior. Finally, it was a 2-year study that engaged 10 students in a meaningful way, and it was a real-world local problem, open ended, with no real right answers. Science came alive for them.

Without examining, creating, and implementing new models for educational opportunity, this experience would not have been possible in a traditional high school. The problem was a science problem, but it quickly developed a social and political side. The research became the students' to own and theirs to defend. In collaboration with mentors and teachers, they designed, implemented, adjusted, and communicated it. They built it and took ownership of it. The project became rich with opportunities for all student ability and motivation levels. This is one example of a long-term project done within a local setting, with local community professionals, that brought meaning to the students' classroom experiences. Following are examples of other project relationships.

The University of California—
Bodega Marine Laboratory and Reserve

The Bodega Marine Laboratory and Reserve is a field station and a satellite campus of the University of California, Davis. Its primary mission is to provide facilities for research and education. The areas of research being done here range in scale from molecular to cellular and include research at the organismal and ecological levels. The reserve portion of the site covers 361 acres of coastal prairie, dunes, rocky and sandy intertidal zones, mudflats, and salt and freshwater marshes that provide opportunities for a variety of field studies.

Studies are a mix of basic and applied research. The facility serves researchers, undergraduates, and graduate students. Students have been able to design and complete research with the help of various mentors at the lab for the past 4 years. In this case, a relationship was developed with a single person at the lab who had a personal interest in education of this type. He has personally facilitated what it has become today. Others at the lab have contributed in many ways within their personal comfort level. Occasionally, university students will work with our students. Some act directly as mentors, some help out for short periods of time, and others are there for advice only. Each contact is unique, and students are carefully matched with mentors and projects. In some cases, the nature of the research is something that the researcher is interested in but does not have the time to do personally.

Today, I have 11 students working there. Their project research is as follows:

1. Ranking order and social structure of a Harbor Seal haul-out site: Are there patterns?
2. Predator/prey relationships between the introduced Atlantic Green Crab and the local indigenous crabs: Are they prey or predator?

3. Studies contrasting and comparing botanical fresh-water seep communities with the areas around them: How unique and different are they?
4. Do tidepool communities reflect and support Island Biogeography Theory?
5. Fouling of marine communities and paint toxicity: Are there environmentally safer paint additives to prevent fouling?
6. Two students are using the current molecular biology research being done at the lab as the subject of a video production to teach the techniques that scientists use to answer questions on the molecular scale.

Most of the expansion and growth of our program has been handled informally as trust has developed and protocols have been established. Parents and students are always asked to come for a tour of the facilities before research begins. Hazards and limits are identified, defined, and discussed. We try to match the projects with a family's ability to support the student. If a student will be leaving campus and driving to the lab, appropriate district forms will need to be signed by the parents. We do have two cold water aquariums in the classroom that, in some cases, reduce the student's need to be at the lab, thereby reducing transportation problems.

The Broadmoor Project

This was a mentored project that included all of my Honors Biology students. The scope of the project covered a large content area, and it became the focus of class activities for 75% of the semester. We considered it an educational experiment. First, let me describe the project. Broadmoor North is a 14-acre parcel of land that our school district purchased as compensation for covering over wetlands on a building site for a new city high school. It also was purchased as a condition for the issuance of a building permit for the new high school for the district. The high school building site included wetlands of questionable habitat value. The Army Corps of Engineers issued a permit for their destruction only after the district agreed to purchase the Broadmoor site as compensation. The Broadmoor site contains wetland and uplands. Portions of the Broadmoor wetland are considered unique and include rare vernal pools. The Army Corps also required the district to draft and implement a 5-year monitoring and vernal pool enhancement plan. That is where we came in. Rather than having district-hired consultants do the required biological and hydrological studies, we, as a class, would do it.

The site is very pristine in comparison to the land around it. It contains two rare or endangered species, one plant and one amphibian. There are a variety of native wildflowers and grasses on the site. It also contains a broad age and size range of Valley oaks. Around our area, there are many large oaks but very few that are medium or small. Many of the younger-generation oaks have been cleared for pasture or farm land. Broadmoor North is a small piece or relic of the original oak savannah that once covered the area.

The permit required a plan to improve the aquatic habitat value for the rare and endangered species. Baseline biological data had to be gathered as a control or comparison to measure changes in site biology after the proposed changes in hydrology were made. The idea was to increase the flow of water to the site, thus increasing the size and number of the vernal pools, which would increase habitat for the rare and endangered species in addition to other wetland organisms. The bottom line is that the site was rich in biological and hydrological field study opportunities. The work was required to be authentic and was to be completed at a professional level required by the Army Corps.

We worked directly and indirectly with a wetlands specialist who oversaw the work. Other consultants included a hydrologist, a botanist, and an ecologist who helped us daily with experimental design, standardizing methods, data collection, and statistics. There were also two community volunteers, people with special interests and knowledge about the site who added their personal expertise and a historical background. Research and baseline data were needed to meet Army Corps conditions. There were also other areas of research that were identified as worthwhile, even if they were not necessary for the report. Research tasks were identified, and students were given their choice of tasks based on their interests. Groups were then balanced, and students developed individual responsibilities within the larger research projects.

First, students, along with mentors and teachers, were asked to design and develop methods within the portfolio format to meet project requirements. These were reviewed by mentors and implemented or revised as necessary. There were many revisions because some projects worked well and others did not. One major project, hydrology, came to an end simply because we had a dry winter and spring with nothing to monitor. Researchers in that group made a shift to soil testing, which turned out to be of real interest. Vernal pool soils are unique. Increasing the amount of water may not increase the size of the vernal pools if the water percolates away. Soils are an important part of the structure. The soil data brought up questions about the potential expansion of wetlands. Mentors and teachers taught and embedded biology content as necessary to understand the nature of research and the site.

Liability waivers were created for student drivers, and for a few weeks, the class traveled to and met at the site. C-TEC has a modified block schedule that allowed the blocks of time necessary. Students created brochures to help educate the neighbors. We gave presentations to the Sierra Club and other organizations. A survey group completed a grid on the site with benchmarks and markers for relocating study sites, and an aerial photography company donated photos and other mapping services. The local paper featured the project in an article.

The project was very worthwhile, and we will continue it. Now that the project is well developed, we will not need as much class time to continue it.

Nonpoint Pollution Project

Nonpoint pollution is roughly described as any pollution that is washed into the storm drains from surface water runoff and not treated or removed at a sewage treatment plant. Some professionals or agencies estimate that as much as 50% of contaminants in city, urban, rural, and agricultural wastewater comes from nonpoint sources and is not treated or removed before entering natural waterways and other bodies of water. This includes runoff from streets, parking lots, and building surfaces.

This project originally was introduced by a parent who happened to be an engineer and owned an engineering firm in town. He knew the Environmental Protection Agency was soliciting grant proposals for various research and other activities related to nonpoint water pollution. The $90,000 grant was designed to provide opportunities for cities to develop a nonpoint pollution mitigation test site and a public education plan to reduce nonpoint pollution. Ultimately, the grant was cowritten by our city's Department of Public Works, the Regional Water Quality Control Board, and our school. Mentors from these agencies supported and guided all aspects of the project. The mitigation test site, with its related technology, was installed and tested at Piner High School. Surface runoff from our site was trapped and treated in collectors installed on our site. The public education component was designed, developed, and implemented with the help of a local TV station and water agency. Student groups in a project class did the science and some of the engineering required by the project. Monitoring was implemented by gathering data needed to rate the effectiveness of the technology. Students started an education group to inform other students at the elementary schools. Others designed and produced brochures to be included in local water bills, and a nonpoint pollution video was produced and shown on local TV. All of this work was structured within the portfolio format.

The Criminal Law Project

The criminal law project uses our criminal justice system as a classroom. This project was created and implemented by a government and history teacher and uses a portfolio format to structure student experiences in preparation for mock trial competitions. The court system is used as a vehicle for motivating students to learn and experience the reality of our court system. Students focus on learning the skills necessary to become successful in mock trials. Frequent courtroom visits become models for learning and developing an understanding for the processes necessary for successful intellectual arguments and clear communication. Lawyers and judges become mentors and foster year-long relationships with students. They help students learn the details of the justice system and gain insight and a working knowledge of the court system. Students are made aware of court cases available on project days and pick the cases most relevant to them and their potential roles in the mock trials. Like the other project examples, students leave campus and arrange, with parental support, trips to the courtroom.

Accountability is based on journal entries and other activities. Behavior problems are eliminated by not allowing students to participate in off-campus activities if problems occur. The week-to-week courtroom visits become lessons and preparation for the mock trials in which the students will engage. The responsibility is placed on the students to learn and practice the skills and protocols necessary for the mock competitions. These mock trials serve as a demonstration of mastery of the courtroom roles the students assume.

The project has many hidden benefits. There are many career and professional choices in the court system, and students see and experience them firsthand. The courtroom drama also becomes a sociology and psychology lesson. Like all of the other projects, the focus is not on the final result; it is the responsibility to the project and the process of preparation that we want the students to experience and master.

The "Steelhead in the Classroom" Project

We are lucky to have a river near our school that still acts as a home for native salmon and steelhead trout. There is even a state-run hatchery nearby. A local chapter of Trout Unlimited has been involved in a program of donating steelhead trout eggs and loaning aquariums to local classrooms for a number of years. The eggs mature and hatch while members work with students on fish and stream ecology and restoration. The fish act as the focal point and create the interest and motivation to learn more. The end of the project comes with a creek walk and the release of the young fish.

We have taken the project a step further by training our high school students to mentor elementary classrooms in the "Steelhead in the Classroom" project. They spend the first semester preparing themselves to adapt a classroom and take responsibility for the entire curricular unit. Their education director acts as a mentor and resource. Education directors provide refrigerated tanks, hatchery contacts, and other necessary equipment and supplies. They also take our students out to the river and creeks to familiarize them with the habitat. For students, this means learning creek ecology and fish biology and creating materials to aid in classroom presentations. It also means contacting and networking with prospective teachers, setting up aquariums, and arranging field trips. Their portfolios reflect preparation events, curricular support material production, contacts with teachers and hatchery personnel, and a learning timetable for project literacy.

The whole project is based on the spawning season of the fish, the number of returning fish, and the availability of eggs. Weather plays a large part in the life cycle of the fish, and sometimes students are at the mercy of the rainy season for the return of the fish.

Science is the obvious topic here, but it goes well beyond the science. Classroom presentations, teaching, and learning the topic well enough to assume an "expert" role make up a true challenge for students. This is one of the founding projects, and it has been in the project program for 5 years.

The Computer Network Project

This was a small project class that was created to fill a specific need within our small school community. We have six classrooms networked with 10 to 15 computer terminals each. There are many programs and files stored on a common file server. Most rooms have a variety of computer types, power, and memory. With no funds for maintenance, training student computer technicians to keep the network up and running became a necessity. Each group has a mix of grades and ages to maximize the students-teaching-students idea. A local computer hardware store donates one of their technicians for an afternoon a week to aid the project. When not doing repair work, building new computers, or programming, students are free to develop their own computer application projects within the class structure. The role of the portfolio changes a bit here. It still may reflect the design and development of a computer class "product," but it is used mainly as a record of growth and accountability for assessment purposes.

In other computer-related projects, an author of computer applications manuals and books runs a "Q" Basic programming class. We also have a math teacher who is also a musician directing a computer music project. Various computer music applications are used to produce original compositions.

Journalism

Journalism is one of the original project-type activities. It is the practical application of the communication techniques learned in English classes. This group usually takes it a step further by completing intermediate projects within the school and community. Students document many other projects; produce CD-ROMs as part of a statewide project; and create, design, and develop many of the materials that are used to communicate activities within the school. Various mentors have created roles within this project for themselves.

10

In Conclusion:
The Future of the Classroom
in the Community

We started with the initial premise that the community offered opportunities for the formation of highly motivating learning opportunities for students and teachers. The curricular style that was presented stresses an open-ended model of problem-based learning, in which the students are free to work within their ability, interest, and motivational levels. The general idea within this program is to give the classroom curriculum validity, relevance, and context. Also, it seeks to foster or instill a sense of self-motivation and self-direction so necessary in high-achieving, active learners.

In a sense, these ideas are not new. In the past, trade apprentice programs and current vocational programs have provided authentic context and a purpose for learning and knowing the techniques and information associated with those trade or specialty areas. Finding formal contacts or creating similar connections in today's academic curriculum and programs is a bit more rare. The cycle of educational design turns around and recycles old ideas, adds new twists and innovations, and applies them to meet the unique needs of today's learners. The bottom line is that the concept of a mentor and community program is as open ended as the projects described in this book. Opportunities are limited only by the imagination of those looking for these types of connections. In fact, more and more grants and funding opportunities that support and facilitate the development of these connections exist than ever before.

As I read the front page of the paper today, I see that a few local science students have made it to the semifinals of the Westinghouse Science Competition. Each student related the evolution of his or her specific project, and all credited various professor-researchers at a local university for their support. The nature and requirements of each project far exceeded their high school's ability to provide support. They needed long-term relationships and resources, and they could not have done it without their mentors. The students became academic apprentices. In most cases, the students or their parents found their own connections. These types of connections should be available to all students, teachers, and classes.

Another college just received a $1 million Howard Hughes grant to create connections to local high schools that will allow "at-risk" students to do molecular biology work under the mentorship of college faculty. The idea is to engage these students in a high-powered program and revitalize their interest and motivational levels in school. A biotech firm outfitted vans with science technologies that travel to various school sites to bring state-of-the-art models of research and investigative pathways wrapped around their real design and development projects. In other examples, some high schools have actually moved some of their programs onto college or university campuses in order to use the resources the host school offers. In another case, a large corporation created space for a small school on the site of their research and development facility. These are all versions of community programs.

The beauty of being an educator today is that we have the opportunity to create programs on-site that make the best use of the resources available to us. The opportunities for creative expansion of these programs and for the creation of new community learning models are open ended and limited only by our imaginations. It is hoped that the ideas and experiences presented here can become a seed of inspiration and a source of the information and intellectual tools that curricular program designers require to meet the needs of future students and educators.

Appendix:
Sample Project Descriptions
for Students and Parents

Project Description for the
University of California, Davis
Bodega Marine Laboratory and Reserve

General Background

The Bodega Marine Laboratory and Reserve (BML) at UC Davis offers students a wide variety of projects and experiences. Past BML projects have been some of our most successful. Projects have the potential to focus on many areas in the biological sciences. The reserve and laboratory cover 361 acres of coastline and harbor, which offers students the opportunity to do both original and valuable types of field and laboratory research. Also, certain organisms may be collected and returned to school and maintained in the classroom. This reduces the travel time to and from the coast. Students are free to collaborate with the mentors and teachers to develop their own projects or further develop continuing or existing projects. We have parent and student orientations and visitations for their introduction to BML and to help define and choose an appropriate research project.

For the fourth year, Victor Chow, PhD, will act as a mentor and facilitator for BML student projects. He is an ecologist and teacher and is also responsible for many of the computer applications at BML. There are also many other teachers and researchers willing to work with students on projects within their expertise. Students considering careers in science or attending the University of California as science majors would especially benefit from this project experience.

Special Requirements and Time Commitment

Time and commitment are the biggest requirements. Round-trip from Santa Rosa to the laboratory is 45 miles. This takes a special commitment from parents, and the selection of a BML project should be well thought out. Trips to the coast can be minimized by collecting organisms and maintaining the project within the classroom. Students with other commitments (work, sports, etc.) would have to make their project their first priority.

Participants should recognize that field research of this nature can be tedious and physically demanding at times. There are few hazards, but researchers need to be aware and exercise reasonable care and caution in some areas. In many cases, data will have to be collected during all weather conditions or at low tides only. Data collection will need to take place at times that may not be convenient for students or parents. We expect researchers to be energetic, self-motivated, precise, meticulous, responsible, patient, and cooperative. Writing skills, record keeping, and computer experience are important to these types of projects.

Project Description for
Broadmoor North Wetlands, Vernal Pools,
and Endangered Species Project

General Background

The Santa Rosa School District owns 14 acres of wetlands in southeast Santa Rosa that provide a habitat for many interesting organisms, some of which include two endangered plant and animal species. The overall goal of the Broadmoor project is to enhance and monitor the existing wetlands, specifically the vernal pools on the site. Increasing the aquatic habitat values will improve conditions for all wetland species. This in turn will increase and enlarge the habitat for the two endangered species on the site, the Sebastopol Meadowfoam and the California Tiger Salamander. Also included as a project goal is recording the decease of nonnative plants and the improvement of the Valley oak habitat. Students will be responsible for the design and development of field study methods to survey existing conditions, and they will continue to monitor on-site changes as improvements are made. Early in the study, students will establish baseline data collection techniques and change them as necessary to collect required data.

The 1993-1994 Honors Biology class began this project and completed some of the preliminary work. This is a 5-year project, and there are numerous opportunities for students to design and develop many interesting studies or continue established research as they learn biology. This project provides researchers with the opportunity to work with wetland scientists and a rare and sensitive habitat within their own community.

Special Requirements and Time Commitment

There will be weekly class time dedicated to this project. However, the nature of the project requires that data on the site be collected during periods of rain and poor weather. Also, some specific projects may require 24-hour attention during limited rainy periods or when water pools on the site. Plants bloom during certain periods, and the Tiger Salamander comes out only during rainy weather. Data collection may not be at the convenience of the student researcher. Specific projects or problems require different types of commitments. It is your responsibility to be clear on the requirements and responsibilities and share these with your parents. Transportation to the site will need to be a shared responsibility. Because of the authentic need for data for a report to the Army Corps of Engineers, students will need to make the project their first priority.

Example of a Parent Letter and Release

September 9, 1994

Dear Parents,

This year, as a member of C-TEC, your son or daughter will be participating in a project class three times a week. For some of the project classes, it will be necessary for the students to travel off campus to various other sites. Students will need to drive themselves or carpool with other students to these off-campus sites. It is very important that you are aware of this aspect of your son's or daughter's project and that we have your permission for your child to drive or ride with another student.

Project classes are on Tuesday from 10:36 am to 12:30 pm, Wednesday from 2:06 pm to 3:00 pm, and Thursday from 1:06 pm to 2:30 pm. On Thursday, lunch starts at 12:30, so some students may leave campus at that time to be able to arrive at their site earlier.

Please discuss with your child the importance of safety and good conduct when he or she leaves campus. Also, talk about where he or she is going, what he or she is doing, and what he or she is learning when off campus.

Thank you for your cooperation.

The C-TEC Project Class Teachers

Required Parental Permission Form

I have reviewed and understand the conditions of the off-campus trip described above and give my consent for my son or daughter to participate. In addition, I am aware of Education Code Section 1081.5, which provides that all people making a field trip or an excursion are deemed to have waived all claims against the school district for injury, accident, or illness occurring during or by reason of the trip. I also give my permission for my son or daughter to be transported by another student or teacher to this school-sponsored activity. IN CASE OF AN EMERGENCY, I AUTHORIZE THAT MY SON OR DAUGHTER BE TAKEN TO THE NEAREST MEDICAL CENTER FOR TREATMENT, IF I AM UNAVAILABLE.

_____

(Signature of Parent)   (Date)

(_____)_____ (_____)_____

(Emergency daytime and home phone numbers)

For the Parents of Students Who Will Be Driving

I certify that the vehicle that will be used for school purposes will be covered by private automobile insurance, in the limits meeting the following requirements: $50,000-$100,000 Bodily Injury, $25,000 Property Damage, and $10,000 Medical. I understand that there will be no school or district insurance that will cover the student or any passenger in the event of an accident.

_____

(Signature of Parent)   (Date)

**CORWIN
PRESS**

Made in the USA
Lexington, KY
16 June 2011